SAINTS AND STRANGERS

THE HOUGHTON MIFFLIN
NEW POETRY SERIES

SAINTS AND STRANGERS

ANDREW HUDGINS

With an Introduction by
JOHN FREDERICK NIMS

HOUGHTON MIFFLIN COMPANY
Boston 1985

Library of Congress Cataloging in Publication Data

Hudgins, Andrew.
    Saints and strangers.
    (The Houghton Mifflin new poetry series)
    I. Title. II. Series.
PS3558.U288S2 1985   811'.54   85-14734
ISBN 0-395-39384-1
ISBN 0-395-39383-3 (pbk.)

Printed in the United States of America

Q 10 9 8 7 6 5 4 3 2 1

ACKNOWLEDGMENTS

Grateful acknowledgment is made to the following magazines in which some of the poems here were first published: The Antioch Review: "On Sentimentality." The American Poetry Review: "The Bog of the Fathers," "Claims," "Sotto Voce." The Georgia Review: "Holofernes Reminisces after Three Thousand Years." The Hudson Review: "The Stoker's Sunday Morning." Intro 13: "Something Wakes Me Up." The Kenyon Review: "Consider," "One of Solomon's Concubines, Dying, Exults in Her Virginity." The Massachusetts Review: "My Father's House." The Missouri Review: "Saints and Strangers." The New Yorker: "Awaiting Winter Visitors: Jonathan Edwards, 1749." The North American Review: "Magnolias." The Ontario Review: "Fire and St. Francis." Ploughshares: "Mary Magdalene's Left Foot." Poetry: "Air View of an Industrial Scene," "Audubon Examines a Bittern," "My Mother's Hands," "Madonna of the Pomegranate," "Julia Tutwiler State Prison for Women," "Sentimental Dangers." Poetry Northwest: "Two Worlds of Sleep," "Amen." The Southern Review: "Sidney Lanier in Montgomery: August 1866," "Walking the Idiots," "Zelda Sayre in Montgomery: 1942." New England Review: "Returning Home to Babylon." The Northwest Review: "Late Spring in the Nuclear Age."

    I would like to thank the University of Iowa, Stanford University, and the Corporation of Yaddo for fellowship assistance while I was writing this book.

For my father and the memory of my mother

CONTENTS

INTRODUCTION

The work of Andrew Hudgins first caught my eye a few years ago, when, as editor of a poetry magazine, I came across a submission with the title "Julia Tutwiler State Prison for Women." My interest in the poet quickened as I read. The scene is stark enough, with its pair of women in green prison clothes on the "tramped-hard Alabama clay," out for as much of a promenade as the chain-link fence allows them. Likely enough they earned their imprisonment by some vivid crime of passion. And yet a kind of sweetness softens the poet's focus on the couple strolling hand in hand. The summer raindrops begin to fall, and, breaking into laughter, still hand in hand, the women race as children might for shelter. With the prison poem was a second one, "Air View of an Industrial Scene." That scene appears innocent, with its train discharging travelers, its tall chimneys and their lackadaisical smoke, its neat garden where someone on his knees is fingering the yellow blooms, his fingers cool in the earth. But suddenly the realization: this is a concentration camp, and the industry is death. We, in the airplane above, are helpless spectators, as so many others had been when even closer to such scenes.

For its epigraph, *Saints and Strangers* has a quotation from St. Augustine: "To blame the fault of a creature is to praise its essential nature." There are few poems here in which the fault or failure of the human creature is not chillingly apparent. Bodies of violated girls are found in the underbrush:

> It's boys who find the bodies in the woods
> and mostly boys who put them there.

ix

Drunken drivers aim — or so it seems to pedestrians on rainy nights — at walkers along the highway. A sleeper wakens to strange sounds; peering out the window he sees hunters butchering, with gruesome detail, a doe they have hung from a child's swing set. For their amusement, boozy sailors trap buzzards and then soak them in kerosene, set them afire, and launch them into the evening sky like living fireworks.

And so on. But invariably the tone is compassionate rather than denunciatory. There is also plenty of reason to praise, with St. Augustine, the essential nature of a creation with such creatures in it. Helpless to do anything about the butchered doe, the observer feels united with humanity in his need to "ask forgiveness." He feels that need even more strongly, of course, when the victims are young girls, their bodies carried off with more gentle concern than if they were alive:

> . . . I love those girls,
> those dead strangers, more than I love anyone . . .

So too with other evils, which, paradoxically, are seen as reasons for understanding, compassion, and atonement in a universe that is never itself evil.

It is, in fact, a universe inexhaustibly generous. In the first poem, "The Persistence of Nature in Our Lives," we see the forest lavishing its infinity of pollen on everything, until, one morning, the floor of the house and the lawn outside are all a green-gold splendor — everywhere except where the fuddled sleeper has left his

> . . . man-shape on the hard
> wood floor, outlined in pollen — a sharp
> spread-eagle figure drawn there like
> the body at a murder scene.

There are lighter touches, too, touches that remind us of Robert Frost when he writes "Spring is the mischief in me" and that use mischief to make a serious point. So in the poem about the pollen that falls alike on the fertile and the barren:

> The pollen settles on my skin
> and waits for me to bloom, trying
> to work green magic on my flesh.
> They're indiscriminate, these firs.
> They'll mate with anything. . . .
> . . . .
> The pollen doesn't care I'm not
> a tree. The golden storm descends.

So too in "Mary Magdalene's Left Foot," in which an illustration in a popular news magazine shows the bogus relic "encased in antique gold / and pedestrian prose." But here also there is an otherworldly seriousness, as the poem ends with "the whore who washed Christ's feet with tears" knowing, as she kissed the bruises and abrasions,

> . . . that it was God's clear flesh beneath
> its human dying. And that is more than you or I
> will ever know of where we place our lips.

There is a bittersweet tenderness in "Sotto Voce," a playful gravity in "Fire and St. Francis," in which the affectionate saint lets himself be scorched by Brother Fire, whose pretty flames he does not wish to disturb as they eat through his robe to his flesh; he is saved only when his companions, more down-to-earth, tackle him like a quarterback to smother the fire.

A heartbreaking confusion between the ridiculous of this world and the sublime of another gives plangency to these poems. We feel it when a painter, forking up lily clumps in her garden, comes up with

> a toad hung limply from the tines. I wept.
> It looked just like El Greco's Christ. The legs.

In "The Bog of the Fathers," Carl Jung dines with Sigmund Freud and talks all through the meal about the bodies of bog men preserved in northern Europe, how only their skin is left, "some brown sacks, / empty and lewdly human." Freud, who senses hostile implications in the way Jung rattles on, suddenly collapses in a faint (he is indeed on record as having done so).

Saints and Strangers — in this impressive first book there are few saints in a world in which we are all strangers. "Stranger" has its Biblical overtones: "stranger in a strange land"; "I was a stranger, and ye took me in." The word recalls too the advice of Thomas à Kempis: "Keep yourself a stranger and pilgrim upon earth." The themes of saint and stranger are nowhere more closely intertwined here than in the final sequence of eight poems, which give the book its title. In these the speaker is a girl growing up with memories of her father, an impassioned revivalist preacher. She remembers how he was beaten by drunken hunters before his own congregation; how, with sorrowful understanding, he found her, a naked twelve-year-old, gamboling in the baptismal font with her young playmates; how he disapproved when her no-good boyfriend, who sang "Amazing Grace" like Donald Duck, kissed her in church. She dwells powerfully on her father's last years, troubled not only by incontinence and the glossolalia brought on by a stroke but also by visions of demons crowding into his environment:

> Strangeness is part of it. And rage and will.
> There's something noble in that suffering
> and something stupid too. . . .

A closer acquaintance with this final group is something I recommend. Here, even more than in the other poems, readers are likely to find something as close to nobility as we can hope to know amid the paradoxical strangeness of our lives.

— *John Frederick Nims*

To blame the fault of a creature
is to praise its essential nature.

— *St. Augustine*

I

The Persistence of Nature in Our Lives

You find them in the darker woods
occasionally — those swollen lumps
of fungus, twisted, moist, and yellow —
but when they show up on the lawn
it's like they've tracked me home. In spring
the persistence of nature in our lives
rises from below, drifts from above.
The pollen settles on my skin
and waits for me to bloom, trying
to work green magic on my flesh.
They're indiscriminate, these firs.
They'll mate with anything. A great
green-yellow cloud of pollen sifts
across the house. The waste of it
leaves nothing out — not even men.
The pollen doesn't care I'm not
a tree. The golden storm descends.
Wind lifts it from the branches, lofts
it in descending arches of need
and search, a grainy yellow haze
that settles over everything
as if it's all the same. I love
the utter waste of pollen, a scum
of it on every pond and puddle.
It rides the ripples and, when they dry,
remains, a line of yellow dust
zigzagging in the shape of waves.
One night, perhaps a little drunk,
I stretched out on the porch, watching

the Milky Way. At dawn I woke
to find a man-shape on the hard
wood floor, outlined in pollen — a sharp
spread-eagle figure drawn there like
the body at a murder scene.
Except for that spot, the whole damn house
glittered, green-gold. I wandered out
across the lawn, my bare feet damp
with dew, the wet ground soft, forgiving,
beneath my step. I understood
I am, as much as anyone,
the golden beast who staggers home,
in June, beneath the yearning trees.

Claims

It's boys who find the bodies in the woods
and mostly boys who put them there.
At cowboys and Indians — a murder game —
they found two naked, dead, and rotting girls
covered with leaves and brush — not even dirt.
I let them use my phone and washed away
their surface grime and fascinated tears.
One, dropping with an arrow in his chest,
had pitched, face-first, into a corpse.
I didn't think to make the call myself.
They knew from television what to do.

All afternoon and into night, a red light
splashed across my whitewashed walls, as men
tramped through the woods to bring the bodies out.
They worked as gently as they could,
more gentle than they'd be with living girls,
because the flesh dissolves at a careless touch
as if to say, *You have no claim on me.*

When they came to ask me what I knew
I didn't know a thing, but wanted to so bad
I had to watch my tongue for fear
that I'd invent a clue to help them out:
a car door slamming shut, a scream at night —
anything to prove I wasn't sleeping.
But what claim do I have to all this guilt
that I've stockpiled like weaponry?

One day as I stared from the kitchen window
I saw a sparrow plunge from the power line
and tumble through my pyracantha bush.
Though I was just a witness to its death
I felt, in some vague way, responsible.
And that was for a bird. What is my guilt?
That I was on the scene and didn't know.

And sometimes when I've drunk too much
and I'm having trouble sleeping, I love those girls,
those dead strangers, more than I love anyone,
even my mother or my dad — both dead —
but dead so long I've lost my hold on them.
The girls also are turning into nothing.
At dawn their eyes struggle for more darkness,
at night their lost breath tangles in the breeze,
and somewhere deeper in the labyrinth of days
there's the sound of an opening being opened.

The Choice the Driver Makes

Their headlights slash across my face and chest
and then the cars surge past, tires sizzling
in the thin drizzle. I don't interest them
as I trudge through the tall wet grass beside
the road. I give them lots of room. It's late.
The drunks are out. And in work pants and dark shirt,
both drenched with rain, I am invisible
until the harsh lights choose me out of night
then blast into the further dark and drop me back
into darkness and give me back my sight.
Two lights veer off the road and aim at me.
For a long moment I stand judging them
almost convinced they'll swerve away, then leap
full-length into wet grass, wholeheartedly,
and cannot tell what choice the driver makes.

Something Wakes Me Up

Something wakes me up. I sit and listen.
A soggy rasp. A pause. Another rasp.
Someone is sawing. Not wood: it's too soft for wood.
There are two of them. They're trying to be quiet,
whispering but loudly. I part the blinds and look.
They've got it strung up from the swing set,
tongue bulging out, eyes huge with gravity.
They rinse her abdomen with a garden hose,
the water's hard stream ringing in the carcass.
Disturbed, I lie back down and close my eyes.
But once I know what's going on outside
each noise explains itself. I've done this before:
sat and listened to men do what I've imagined,
and not know how to stop them or turn them in.
The rasp returns — a higher pitch. They're sawing off
the hooves. And worst of all: long shearing rips
as they tear the skin from the tendons and yellow fat.
Then sawing again. Long sinking strokes: the head.
With hammer and chisel they split her down the spine
and toss the doe meat in their pickup trucks.
It's quiet. The muscles of my neck relax.
And I get up and write it all to you
as a stronger man might simply ask forgiveness.

In the Night Garden

It's cooling down — summer
somehow leaving with daylight,
and after dark the bees

no longer fumble against
the flowers. Oh, there was one
buzzing, caught inside

a squash flower, but I
pinched the soft trap open
and let it go. Around me

the night bugs are coming out.
They love the beans. Right now
they are turning

the heart-shaped leaves into
lacework — delicate
even frilly, like the scissored

snowflake of a careful child.
The peppers glisten in
the moonlight but they would glisten

anywhere — a closet, a cave.
They make their own light.
A breeze, and the tomatoes bobble,

creaking their wire cages.
I've used these cages
seven years, each spring tossing

them, crushed, out of the shed
and pulling them back
into shape. For seven years

I've watched the loaded vines
sag the wire. I snap a green
tomato from the vine, thinking

that tomorrow I will slice it,
dip the slices in egg, then
cornmeal, and fry them

for my wife and me. But tomorrow
is not one of the days
she spends with me. I toss

the hard tomato in the air
and catch it, slapping my palm
up hard into its fall;

it is still warm with the day's
sun. The squash look
like pale light bulbs, but

the eggplants are hard to see.
Pendant and almost fleshy
they grow out of night

itself, its purple air,
its heart that can't quite
blacken. Soon, I'll walk to the house

and sleep beside my sleeping
wife. Then I'll wake early
— while it's still dark — and return

to this garden and these fruits, which
I will gather and eat —
or give away. But I have,

at times, late in the summer,
let the tomatoes go through
their cycle. They split and ooze,

then come apart. The seeds
fall away. Some people take
comfort in this — not me.

I work the garden for
the eating and the giving away.
When I come back here, I

will hunker, crouch really,
in the silence of plants, things
that move so slowly

they can be called
inanimate. I'll be here when
she leaves for work. Her bare

legs will flash like scissors
in the sun. Or maybe
I will stay in bed until

she's gone. I love to sleep
and I refuse to be the hero
or the villain of my life.

Mary Magdalene's Left Foot

I saw the picture in *Newsweek* or *Time*
and couldn't believe who was back in the news.
But there it sat, encased in antique gold
and pedestrian prose, apart from the rest
of her imaginably lush lost body,
which it recalls with false synecdoche.

The news is littered with the bodies of women
— whores, some — who have returned to minerals,
a pile of iron and zinc and calcium
that wouldn't even fill a shoe. We glimpse
of Mary Magdalene a golden whole
that never ached for flesh or grew hair coarse
enough to scrub mud from a traveler's foot.

But gold is meretricious flattery
for the whore who washed Christ's feet with tears,
who rubbed sweet oil into his sores, then kissed
each suppurating wound that swelled his flesh,
knowing that it was God's clear flesh beneath
its human dying. And that is more than you or I
will ever know of where we place our lips.

Sentimental Dangers

When out of work and fierce with self-pity
I'd walk until the fierceness left my feet
and I broke down. Then I'd start home,
where once I walked up to find my wife
pitching a stick across the parking lot
while an ugly dog sat and looked at her.
She'd found him near the office where she typed,
and fed him half her sandwich. He'd hung around
until she'd given in and brought him home.
But he loved me so much that when I went
to play with him, he'd roll onto his back
and piss until it splattered on his chest.
I'd sit outside all afternoon and talk
to him, to the hard knowledge in his face
that she'd leave me when I was well enough
to be left. I talked too much. She'd tell her friends,
He's out of work. He thinks he is that dog.
And she was right, I did. But we were poor,
living on frozen chicken pies and tea —
I knew I'd have to take him to the pound.
As I signed him away with my right hand
and wiped my left — which he would not stop licking —
against the unwashed leg of my blue jeans
I felt I was signing myself away.
An illusion, sure, but one that lasted months.
I thought of this today when I crossed the bridge
and the river smelled like a wet, unwanted dog.

Sotto Voce

I'm standing in the university
library, staring at the German books
and I don't parle eine word of Allemand.
Actually I'm listening to a girl named Beth
call her boyfriend in El Paso.
He's leaving her for work in Mexico
and other reasons. She doesn't understand,
repeats out loud the things he says, as if
the sound of her own voice will help make sense
of what is happening. And even now
her voice is airy, cool, and beautiful;
only her humor perks into uncertainty
as she tries to turn around his serious

long-distance voice. Do you think he can hear
the slender tremolo that plays above
the sureness of her nonchalance?
I thumb through Günter Grass's poems
and watch her pull pink tissues from her purse.
With practiced hands she shreds them into strips
then floats them to the phone booth's tiny floor,
the phone held lovingly between her ear and shoulder.
As if it were already painless, she's
reminding him of the evening they made love
(her alto — half in music — lingers on
the simple words) in her parents' queen-size bed.
The percale sheets were striped yellow and white

and, yes, he remembers. She had to change
the sheets and tell her mother she had read

herself to sleep downstairs, then wet the bed —
her first such accident in eighteen years.
She talks until he starts, I think, to laugh,
and she laughs back in harmony with him,
the laughs oddly resonant though his
is still in Texas and I can't really hear it.
Relaxed at last, her legs slant longly from
the open booth, and I can understand
just why he had to run to El Paso
to leave her. Suddenly she glances up
and I sandwich my head in *The Tin Drum,*

which by a fifty-fifty chance is right
side up. For a few moments more she whispers
into the phone, then stops to listen. *Regret*
is the only word that I can make out clearly,
and even then I can't decide if it's hers
or if she's repeating what he said.
But with a smile she hangs the phone up and
clicks down the hall to the elevator, leaving
the bottom of the booth fluffed with pink tissue.
Over the whole of German literature
I see her smiling, framed in the closing doors;
her afterimage holds the same sure pose,
floating on air, in the empty shaft, and fading.

My Father's House

From a second-story window in my father's house
I see a steeple sway in the evening breeze.
The congregation's moved to a new brick church,
leaving the sagging steeple to the winds and wasps,
and to my father and the other folks
who've come to a random stop beside a church
that cannot mourn them: during the Great War
its bell went the way of many bells
when it was melted for its dollop of metal.
In the growing dark, the window turns
half mirror, a collage of in and out:
my face, the graves, the unhaunted church.
If this were a hundred, or even eighty, years ago
I could hear above the house the bluish peal
of thin bells breaking high on the night.

Two Worlds of Sleep

Someone old has come to live with us,
someone borrowed, someone who
sleeps underneath an open window
of her own, and joins the furnishings of a room
too small for all the sleep it holds.
Beside her bed there stands a child's blue chair
with her dress folded over it.
She wants to go slowly, she wants to know
everything. Grandmothers
practice being their own ghosts,
becoming vague. The sharp features fade,
the dull ones disappear. Before
we know it, she is invisible, known
only by the accidental sounds she makes —
not speech or sounds of pain: the soft bump
of a hip brushing a wall
or the clack of a thick cup knocked off
the kitchen table, as though part of her body
had suddenly returned, surprising her.
And more than once during the Late News,
she has discovered the upright in my bedroom,
pushed back the bedspread covering it,
and slowly picked out "Rock of Ages,"
pressing her fingers into the small pockets
of song. She presses till her fingers hurt.
Then the music pauses, her hands rising over the keys
like an upstroke of wings.
The downstroke is not insisted on.

The Corn Snake

After fishing all morning — not a bite, not one —
I walked from the lake and saw a corn snake,
three foot long, writhing all of its brown-and-yellow
    length except
for one stretch the width of a car tire
as if in that one spot it were pasted to the road,
where in fall, in November, it had crawled from the underbrush
    to the tarmac.
The scales of the flattened stretch were already flaking loose,
    clouding,
death convulsing outward to the head and tail.
The killing itself was mercy
but how I chose to do it — that
was curiosity. I could have ground its skull
beneath my boot heel or slapped its head against a rock;
instead, I grabbed its tail, walked back down to the lake,
the snake twisting weakly in my hand, head knocking at my
    ankle,
the muscles flexing inside the closed muscles of my hand,
and, at the water's edge, snapped my wrist,
looping a sine wave through the vertebrae.
The brains snapped from the skull as if a gun
had gone off in my hand, or a roman candle,
and a pale yellow dollop
arched, fell, and was met by a large bass — prescient, silver —
which rose, struck the disintegrating gob of brain,
and ran with it into the cold beneath the surface,
where I had fished since dawn and caught nothing.

My Mother's Hands

Yawning, she yanks the shuttle through the frame.
It's almost time for lunch. She takes a breath,
and notices her hands curled on the wood.
She sees a basketwork of cool blue veins,
and muscles, and, beneath it all, the bones.
Amazed, she hugs them to her sides, and goes
to tell the boss she's sick. Then she walks home,
gets in the bed she's left unmade, and stays
until she cannot see beneath the skin.

• • •

My mother jerks my sister from the box
and folds her in a bolt of calico,
winding her in a yellow, flowered shroud.
Within each wind, she slaps some jewelry
until she's stripped of any ornament.
She lifts the bundle of my sister up
and with resentment at the letting go
slams it into the short walls of its box.

• • •

My mother sighs and watches television.
Her hands are in the kitchen, washing dishes,
scrubbing their faces with a Tuffy pad,
and stacking them to dry. She sighs again.
She wants an afterdinner cigarette.
They click the final plate against the others.
She glances toward the hands. They dry themselves,
take out the broom, and start to sweep.

• • •

My mother stares into the unused well.
She's pulled aside the curling plywood cover
and puzzles at a gossamer of light
inside the dark. Perhaps a spider web.
Then she removes her tanned, decaying arms
and drops them through the air beneath the ground.
They're so diseased they do not even splash,
and Mother, watching them, is suddenly
struck motionless and never moves again.

Late Spring in the Nuclear Age

FOR CLARE ROSSINI

The fish hit water nymphs, breaking surface.
I hear the splash but when I turn to look
it's gone, the troubled water smoothing itself
back into blue glass. But sometimes I see it,
a bass wrench in midair as it pierces
the membrane of our world. How graceless it is,
the absolute half-second of its flight.

It's hard to say what's different.
It's not the bass. It's not that
I've seen two butterflies poised on one leaf,
their moist wings drying with slow rhythmic flaps.
The leaf quavered beneath their double weight.
Nor that above me on the hill I hear
a small boy hunting in the cemetery.
A hummingbird dissolves in the shotgun blast.
In water oaks the sparrows pause, don't sing,
then one by one their voices catch, unfurl,
as if they had forgotten what they heard.
But that is nothing new. We're used to death —
if not resigned. I stretch here on damp grass,
a paste of seeds and dew smeared on my boots,
trying to move the world into my mind
so I'll have it when summer settles in,
when it's too hot for blossom-set or talk
and nothing moves. This is what's different:
my prayer there'll be a summer to survive,
that our deaths will not be the last.

On Sentimentality

The first time I saw *Limelight*, it didn't move me.
Tereza looks from side to side, her mouth
so far open it overwhelms her face;
she doesn't think to cover it, just stands
in the doorway, distraught, hands lost at her sides.
And then she screams. He's taken his posters,
leaving bright rectangles where they'd hung.
The room is as neat as other people's lives.
I thought the scream was too much, sentimental.
But life doesn't scruple at anything.
Coming home from work, I walked in the door
and fell to my knees. I didn't think to scream.
The pictures were gone and the room was eerily neat
except for a frantic woman who felt she had
to say good-by. And that was all she'd say.
The second time I saw Tereza there,
in the door, her body curved slightly forward in grief,
I felt his absence sinking into her
and thought, *Because she isn't real*
she'll do everything I did and do it better.
She finally understands he's gone. She screams.
We're real, we cannot do it for ourselves.

Prayer

The preacher had us get down on our knees
to pray, our elbows propped on butt-warmed seats.
A woman to my left across the aisle
began to holler, *Hep me, Jesus! Hep
me, Jesus!* And never having seen
a thing like that before, I rose to look.
Without a word, my mother drove her arm
into my side. I doubled up and smacked
my head against the pew. And though it hurt
I had enough sense not to yell or cry.
Years later in a backwoods Baptist church
I heard a woman in great rolling sobs
cry, *Hurt me, Jesus! Hurt me, Jesus Lord!*
and even if he didn't I am sure
that he got credit for an answered prayer.
And later yet, through a gimcrack motel door,
I heard a woman scream, *Fuck me, Jesus!*
Fuck me, Jesus! It must have been a prayer.

•   •   •

My girlfriend called last night at three A.M.
and woke me. She was crying, could hardly talk.
She had been raped when she was seventeen.
She had to tell me. She understood if now
I had to leave her. And all that I could say
was, *No, it doesn't bother me.* A lie.
It sticks like something putrid in my throat
that when I put my hands on friends and say,
Be healed, nobody yet has been healed. Still,

of all the things I've given up to logic
this the last one — prayer — the one I can't
let go, for logic cannot understand
the virtues of a vicious circle, why
a mother suckles her contagious child,
or why the victim has to be rebuked.
And logic doesn't stand a chance, a prayer.

II

Walking the Idiots

It seldom varies. Soon as they're out the door
the tall man wanders off the route to slap,
in joy, a passing mongrel on the head,
then lags behind to watch a tardy bee
fallen in the snow. Its freezing wings

have flailed a narrow tunnel through the flakes
and it lies at the bottom, droning slowly.
The woman doesn't pause, or even look.
She holds her stride and every second step
her torso ticks abruptly to the left.

Between them, hesitant in the widening gap,
the boy makes up his mind, runs down the street.
He slips his hand into the man's slack fist
and they race, hand in hand, for the marching woman.
Dark wings of sweat extend across her blouse.

Her back reminds the boy of finding her
bent to the table, dismantling a toad.
Enraged, he'd slapped her hard across the neck.
She'd sobbed in shock and said between the sobs,
I had to see what made it jump. I had to.

So the boy, curious and because it was already dead,
sat down, and they, with needle and pocketknife,
completely took the toad apart.
When they catch up he grabs the woman's hand —
they all three go careening down the street,

the boy almost suspended from their wrists.
Suddenly the man, excited, spots a lily
brightly alive in the year's first early snow,
and kneels to laugh into the yellow cup.
The quick stop flips the boy across his back.

Confused, he lies a moment in the snow
before he runs to overtake the woman.
She'd bobbed on past, oblivious to them.
He leads her back, kneels in the scanty snow
beside the man, and laughs into the lily.

He feels the laugh reflected on his face,
and laughs again. His knees grow wet, then cold.
He stands, dusts off the snow, and says, *It's late.*
So they start toward the door, a shrinking boy,
two idiots occasionally in hand.

Holofernes Reminisces after Three Thousand Years

Mine is the oldest story
in the world: a man who wields
great power finds the woman
who exists for him to wonder over.

Truly, Assyria, I have no excuses
worth offering;
even now I am moved by
her beauty, inviolate, moist, and Hebrew.

Truly, a woman to astonish!
I was drunk, it is true,
the night she remained in my tent
and I sent the eunuch away.

So I remember only glimpses:
sandals
bracelets
brown flesh

under linen,
and the scent floating over conversation:
perfumed oil, redolent more
of night and body,

more of the hollow of her throat than perfume.
Drunk, Assyria, we exchanged
desires, an old man's night
for a woman's sword.

The world knows only
her side, and in the world mine
is the older story:
a man of merely great power

finds a woman with a gift for doing
what must be done.

Sidney Lanier in Montgomery: August 1866

1.

A walk abroad our Sunday streets
is like a stroll through lost Pompeii,
though our lives aren't so interesting
as theirs, at least as Bulwer-Lytton tells
of them in his book on the last days.
If you went on a Sunday walk with me,
you'd see that almost nothing moves.
The trees stand motionless, like statues,
and even when a breeze steals in,
the leaves flap once, then idly swing
in dull halfhearted protest of
the least disturbance of their rest.
Our weekday streets are much like Sunday's,
so business, as you might expect,
sets no one's heart to fluttering.
I don't believe a man in town
could be induced to go into
his neighbor's store and ask, *How's trade?*
for he would have to make amends
for such an insult all his life.
Even the bugs refuse to move
in all this seething heat. Alone
among insects, the bee — beloved
of Virgil for his industry —
is always busy, foraging
even into the midst of town
and seeking out the last coarse rose
or random violet. But then,
after the bees have ceased their toil,

our streets show no life save late in
the afternoon, when girls come out,
slowly, one by one, and shine and move,
as do the stars an hour later.

2.

I don't intend to quarrel with summer.
This is the first since 'sixty-one
I haven't dressed in butternut.
Yet even in this pastoral land
the green is mixed with battle cries
and phantom groans. A handsome spring
it was. But, my sweet God, to me
the flowers stank of sulphur and
their blooms were flecked with human blood.

At night I think much of the sea.

3.

Come fall I hope to travel north
with the manuscript of *Tiger-Lilies*,
on which I try to work at night,
while moths like dusty knuckles rap
the lighted glass. Before midnight,
when the sultry air is somewhat cooled,
the mockingbirds refuse to sing.
I wait for them. And out my window

the fireflies flicker slower than
I've ever seen those tiny lights.

Our world yawns in a witchery
of laziness. On us is cast
a spell, "an exposition of sleep"
as overtook Sweet Bully Bottom.
The proper term is *aestivation*,
a word that I'm enchanted with.

4.

I've heard they nearly always follow
the river's course — the flaring birds
that arch across the late-night sky
from time to time. I had no way
of guessing what they were: not stars —
though higher than the fireflies rise,
they fly too low for stars. I asked around
and found that drunken sailors set
meat scraps along the riverbanks
and with a crude trap made of rope
ensnare the buzzards they attract.

These birds, kept tied till after dark,
they douse with kerosene, set on fire,
then launch into the evening sky.
The burning makes them fly quite high;
the flying expedites the burning —

it progresses geometrically
until they fall, like burnt-out stars,
into the Alabama River.
One night, preoccupied with work,
I think I made a wish on one.

For them it must be hideous,
but from the ground it's beautiful —
in some odd way an easement of
the savage tedium of days.
But more than that: perhaps you know,
with the younger generation of the South
after the lost war, pretty much
the whole of life has been not dying.
And that is why, I think, for me
it is a comfort just to see
the deathbird fly so prettily.

One of Solomon's Concubines, Dying, Exults in Her Virginity

They tell me it's a fever. So
I'm right again. I burn and burn
and then go cold. And in between
they balance off and I can think
as clearly as I ever have.
A clearing in the brain is like
a clearing in the woods, a place
to stand and watch the circling trees
go up in flames, to study fire
while red and orange swirls close in
on me.

        I came to Israel
at seventeen: an offer made
was ridiculed by his eunuch.
So I was added to a deal
for twenty others, rounding out
the bargain. He always has
a poverty of virgin girls,
for whom he has a private need.

During a childhood fever I
lost all my hair; it grew back white.
One eye turned brown and doesn't work
in concert with the violet one.
Since then I've had a tendency
to fits, a talent I've advanced
till I can see the future like
a master huntsman sees a tiger

crouched in a thicket, while the beaters see
a wall of leaves. Sharp leaves.

He touched my breast and called me sweet.
Then I fell victim to a spell
and called out loudly of a sudden,
Something is burning! He touched me
with practiced hands, firmer this time,
and called me sweet again and said
I was imagining, a common fault
of virgins. *When I tell you some-
thing's burning, something is burning,* I said.
*Something is burning in Israel.
Is it a foreign ship in port,
a mendicant's poor desert fire,
or a stranger's soul I smelled in passing?
It's burning now and will be here
sometime tonight, burnt to a cinder.*
He sent me back and had the eunuch
send up another, calmer virgin.
They brought me to him only once.
If I'd been beautiful or young,
he would have thrown me to the bed
and breached me anyway.

That very night inside the walls
an olive merchant's son burst into flames,
ran shrieking up the midnight streets,
and died not fifty feet from here.

I don't need confirmation for
myself. I've learned to trust my feelings
as they come to me. Yet the thing itself
is nice to flaunt at skeptics like
the king's most trusted eunuch,
whose noncommittal, boy-girl smile
I've seen before on poisonous lizards.

If he, the king, had raped me then,
I would have lost my gift of prophecy —
it's my one small comfort to know,
in some ways, what will happen next.
You've no idea what it does
for a woman's sense of grace to hear
the tune her life's unfolding to.
A temple dancer's poise informs
her body long into marriage
and through the bloody rip of labor.
And even walking, burdened, through
the marketplace, she senses where
to set her feet most gracefully
and how her aging torso sways.
Although it isn't quite the same,
my gift has given me that sense
of knowing things instinctively,
not being taken by surprise.

                    For instance I
have seen the face of my old age

arrange itself as visage on
the mottled back of my brown hand
and known my flesh is wholly mine.
Though I will never live to know
the vision's truth, I've seen that face
smile off my hand at me, and I
have laughed at it and it at me.
Then I have kissed my old age on
the mouth, and it has kissed me back.

The Stoker's Sunday Morning

The curate drones about Abednego,
Shadrach, Meshach, the unnamed fourth,
who stood black and nonchalant
among the ineffectual flames.
He talks as though he daily strolls
through a hell-hot furnace and goes
back home, redolent of ashes and glory.
My hands, as they unfold from morning prayer,
are lined with soot and dark from burning.

At work in the weekday boiler room,
I pile heat on heat in Mississippi,
where there's hardly any need for fire
except two chilly months a year.
The scrape and rise of shovel blade
empties the room into the furnace.
Once in the flames, the coal is beyond sound,
like money, which never even clinks
on the velvet bottom of the offering plate.

The birds outside the stained-glass windows
brawl and copulate beneath the eaves —
what dark spasmodic shapes they make
behind the thieves and bright crucifixion!
I've seen the same vague birds in fire,
and fed the flames they live among.
The curate says he has no doubt
that unaccustomed labor opens up the soul
to awe of ordinary things.

Perhaps in memory. Twelve hours a day
the furnace leaves no time for thought
or mere despair, the sin that claims
much of my time. The rector leads
us in a collect, and then a hymn.
Above me in the cut-glass winter air
the church bell chimes in answer to
our final prayer. Fire, like a choir, can sing,
and water in a pipe will sometimes ring.

Magnolias

Alabama: the first, a girl child.
The rocking chair is cold, the porch colder,
but I could sit here for a year,
thinking of my child, her dwindling.

The magnolias too are windswept
graveward. Neither live oak nor reed
resists the weather's breath,
but each lets go its green, its living part.

Spring, when it comes, is at first wet,
becoming lush, giving way
to the darkgreen darkness
where magnolia leaves hover like wings,
inches off the receding earth.

Then the blooms on the tree will open.
They are so clearly flesh of
our flesh. Without the prolonging bone,
so clearly transitory.

When touched — and I touch them —
the blossoms smudge,
the flesh dying beneath my acid hands,
turning brown in the shape of fingertips.

Fire and St. Francis

1.

As he sat eating by the fire one night
a spark was lifted on a wisp of air
and set on the folds of cloth that wrapped his groin.
But when he felt the heat so near his flesh
he wouldn't raise his hands against the fire
or let his worried friends extinguish it.
You mustn't harm the flames or spoil their play,
he said to them. *Don't these bright creatures have*
as much a right as I to be happy?
For seconds his disciples stared as the flames
climbed up the cloth and nearer to his skin.
And he, without a qualm, turned to his bowl.
At last their knowledge of the world prevailed.
As one, they leapt on him and held him down,
smothering the fire with dirt and what was left
of the soup that had been their evening meal.
When he returned, embarrassed, to his prayers,
his genitals swung through holes scorched in the cloth.

2.

Laid on the fire, the iron throbbed red with heat,
and then turned orange beneath the doctor's breath.
The saint's face twisted in a burst of pain,
and the doctor marked it with a dab of soot
so he would know where to apply the iron.
To calm himself, the saint spoke to the flame:
Brother Fire, be gentle on my quenching skin
that I might have the love to suffer you.

Composed, he signed the cross above the fire,
which bowed its many heads in seeming grace
beneath the blessing motion of his hand.

3.

He held the ember in his hand, and braced.
But soon the burning grew too great to bear,
and Francis set it gently back into the fire
and wept. His hand was oozing from the burn.
A new disciple asked him why he wept
since when you hold an ember in your hand
you know what to expect. Francis wrapped the hand
in a grimy strip of cloth torn from his robe
and said, *When I was young I had a dog*
that snapped my hand whenever I touched him,
and every time he did I held it out again.
About the hundredth time, he licked my wrist.
Perhaps he just grew tired of biting me,
or maybe with my pain I'd earned his trust.
About this fire, however, I don't know.
I dream some day the flames will flit
around my fingers like a yellow bird,
a tulip leaping on my fingertips.
But so far it won't take me for a friend.

Awaiting Winter Visitors: Jonathan Edwards, 1749

When thunder fell in Tinsley's pasture
we recognized a sign from heaven.
From that day on we have rejoyced
that God has not forsaken us:
a blast upon the wavering wheat
is God's lean son walking ghost-
colored through our bodies, saying,
Yours is a famine of the soul.

On my advice the congregation met
six nights a week to pray and sing,
to burn the bushel off our flame.
Beneath a tired December sky
we looked for a descending light
to radiate from New England shores
to the almost mythic cusp of Asia.

Instead, the signs would not form
a prophecy. Attendance fell;
the fervor would not hold its bloom.
In March, hens in the cemetery
pecked up the younger Perkins boy,
who died of pox the winter past.
And yesterday the family cat

ate a poison spider, sickened, died.
I shall miss Joshua. Asleep on my lap
while I composed sermons, he'd purr
like a bit of Satan almost controlled.

At home Sarah's held to the hard faith.
We've supped on vegetables and bones,
but mostly bones, those old friends

returning from other, more fleshy stews.
It built, it built to no climax
then passed to spring — with dandelions
and little purple weeds: the white
fields laced with merciless speedwell.
I shall retire and read St. Paul,
who called the human corpse a seed.

Audubon Examines a Bittern

A lady brought me a Least Bittern
wrapped in her skirt. She woke this morning
to find it perched on her bedpost.
It stuck its beak up in the air
and tried to pretend it was a reed,
a trick that works well on the marsh
but not so well in a lady's bedroom.
I'd only left my window open
a crack, she said, *but there it was.*
It didn't struggle much, scream,
or foul the cloth. (They usually do.)
It posed, beak up, and didn't budge
for ninety minutes while I sketched it.
Then, an experiment of sorts:
I set up books two inches apart
and jabbed the bird with a pencil.
Between my Gray's *Anatomy*
and a large red book about Brazil,
it strolled like a lord on his way to town.
I moved them closer — an inch apart.
The bird was wonderful! It marched right through!
When I killed it, I found its breast
two and a quarter inches wide.
Bedamned if I know what to make of that.

Zelda Sayre in Montgomery: 1942

I've put my easel on the patio
so all I paint is *fleurs*. There's little rain.
It doesn't seem to hurt the flowers though:
azaleas, tulips, japonica, and such.
But the human world is so distressed
I imagine people coming by at night
to yank them up. I see their oblong heads
open with the mad laughter and large eyes
of devils fleeing from a Bosch canvas.
I hear the dry roots tearing from the dirt
like heavy fabric ripped against the grain,
and then there's Easter. I am not ready.
Mother had pyracantha on the table.
Since Christ wore thorns, I made her throw it out.
The scent of pear's been in my room all spring.
The neighbors planted them across the street
when I was twelve. I've loved them ever since
and had worse lovers. None as delicate.

And here is something else I'll never paint:
the cat sits in the window, looking in.
A fat moth flutters gently in his mouth.
Release and catch, release and catch until
he's worried it to pieces — mostly wings —
and still the pieces try to get away.
Sometimes it's birds and even, once, a squirrel.
I've beaten Caesar daily. It does no good.
I'll render unto Caesar, Caesar's things.

I've never painted dogwood. Lack the nerve.

The sprinklers wave above the flawless lawns,
each with its own rainbow, and each rainbow
endowed with all the colors of
the spectrum, visible and invisible.
On the yards, mimosa blossoms mix with grass
as if someone had torn apart flamingos
and spread the bright pink bits across the town.
We had a funny snow this year. March first.
I stood right here and watched an early bee.
The false spring had deceived it, drawn it out.
Its wings had flailed a tunnel through the snow
and it lay at the bottom, droning slowly.
It doesn't take great perspicacity
to see I'm talking — somewhat — of myself.

This morning — Palm Sunday — I woke up early
and wanted to wear silk. Here, that means church.
On the way I stepped into the Parkers' garden,
broke off a calla lily for my hair.
They must have noticed it when I walked up
and knelt to take God's body in my mouth.
They're using sherry now and nasty stuff.
The paper yesterday told of a nun
who, at this time each year, bleeds from her palms.
I've heard of that before, but yesterday
I understood it for the first time ever:

a suffering I could put to use, a hurt
denied to all us doubting Thomases.

I wanted to sleep on the porch. Impossible.
Mosquitoes filled the night with sucking mouths.
They ate me up because I was so fair.
But Father sprayed the air with kerosene
and I slid into a sleep so absolute
I could have been a painting of myself,
my senses stunned with pear and kerosene.
But that was years ago and Father's gone.
This afternoon I used the garden fork
to separate day lilies. I pushed it
under the roots and leaned on it, hard,
to force them up. And when the fork came up
a toad hung limply from the tines. I wept.
It looked just like El Greco's Christ. The legs.

III

Amen

This story begins *Amen*
and ends *Our Father*. It gets

everything backward.
It understands in part if

it understands at all,
but it yearns impossibly for grace

even in its successes.
There is some love

in this story, though not
enough. In that

it is like me and like
life. Though it has rules,

they change.
It digs through grief

with an old shovel, gives up,
burns the shovel, digs with

the ashes. Both ways
the progress is the same

but one way there's light,
the blue talc of ashes

rubbed on the face, and
the brute proximity.

The ashes, thus, come
from burning. Next is the sackcloth,

then
the *Our Father.*

The Bog of the Fathers

In northern Germany the bogs dispense
the modern bodies of prehistoric men,
the corpses lugubriously bobbing up
like a fragile, slow, insistent dream.
And Jung talked of them from first course
to chocolate mousse, waving his teaspoon
in a cheerful maestro's arc before
Freud's more and more unfocused eyes.

Humic acid, he explained, consumes the bones
and tans the skins. And what is left to stink
on the surface of the bog are some brown sacks,
empty and lewdly human. "Sometimes I think,"
he laughed, "that this is the immortal part:
the sausage casing and not the human heart."
At once Freud snapped, "Why do you rattle on
about these things. It proves you wish me dead."
Embarrassed, Jung demurred. A moment later
Freud toppled from his chair in a quick faint,
the great Hebraic brain jarring softly on
the rug of Bremen's finest restaurant.

Once Freud was safely in the grave, Jung struck
from his memoirs: "I shall never forget the look
he cast at me, as if I were his father.
The ten seconds or so he took to float
up through that peculiar public slumber
I held him cradled till he came to —
an awkward pietà: fathers both, sons both.

Our love was never stronger than the moment
it ended. Bog life is brief. Of saurians
all that's left is the wretched crocodile."

Madonna of the Pomegranate

after Botticelli

They crowd the blue triangle of the Madonna —
these adolescents who are also angels,
eyes staring everywhere but straight ahead,
absorbed in the changeless commerce of their world.
They're much like us. Some curiosities.
The wings that curve upward from their backs
are such unwieldy limbs — pure ornament —
you'd know that Botticelli made them up
even if you believed in messengers
with human wings. Where are the muscles
to lift an eighty-pound schoolgirl in the air?
And even if the wings are miracles
how do they get their tunics over them?
But wings aside, the angels look like kids.
One gossips, one has hard, suspicious eyes,
and several wear the slightly stupid look
most children wear when contemplating babies.
Madonna doesn't notice them. She's vague,
thin-faced, eyes drifting downward to the left,
a virgin holding her first child, cradling
him on the tips of her long, fragile fingers
as if she isn't sure where he came from —
so beautiful he almost isn't flesh.
Thus only Christ, unwavering, looks at us,
his left hand resting on a pomegranate
that splashes ruby light into the air,
his right hand raised in blessing or a wave
as he forgives us for not being art
or says good-by since he will live forever.

Julia Tutwiler State Prison for Women

On the prison's tramped-hard Alabama clay
two green-clad women walk, hold hands,
and swing their arms as though they'll laugh,
meander at their common whim, and not
be forced to make a quarter-turn each time
they reach a corner of the fence. Though they
can't really be as gentle as they seem
perhaps they're better lovers for their crimes,
the times they didn't think before acting —
or thought, and said to hell with the consequences.
Most are here for crimes of passion.
They've killed for jealousy, anger, love,
and now they sleep a lot. Who else
is dangerous for love — for love
or hate or anything? Who else would risk
a ten-year walk inside the fenced-in edge
of a field stripped clean of soybeans or wheat?
Skimming in from the west and pounding hard
across the scoured land, a summer rain
raises puffs of dust with its first huge drops.
It envelops the lingering women. They hesitate,
then race, hand in hand, for shelter, laughing.

Air View of an Industrial Scene

There is a train at the ramp, unloading people
who stumble from the cars and toward the gate.
The building's shadows tilt across the ground
and from each shadow juts a longer one
and from that shadow crawls a shadow of smoke
black as just-plowed earth. Inside the gate
is a small garden and someone on his knees.
Perhaps he's fingering the yellow blooms
to see which ones have set and will soon wither,
clinging to a green tomato as it swells.
The people hold back, but are forced to the open gate,
and when they enter they will see the garden
and some, gardeners themselves, will yearn
to fall to their knees there, untangling vines,
plucking at weeds, cooling their hands in damp earth.
They're going to die soon, a matter of minutes.
Even from our height, we see in the photograph
the shadow of the plane stamped dark and large
on Birkenau, one black wing shading the garden.
We can't tell which are guards, which prisoners.
We're watchers. But if we had bombs we'd drop them.

Returning Home to Babylon

The eunuch who loves Daniel — Ashpenaz —
is not alone. It helps to think of him,
the loss he curls around to sleep, and how,
each night, he ushers to the king's bedchamber
a different woman. He watches. He decides
it's like entering a mirror, himself, a thing.
He knows how *other* Daniel is. He has
no choice, and if he did he'd take the whole
surplus of lust that might, perhaps, drive him
to slip alone into the prophet's cell.
He'd press his cheek against the other's cheek
and breathe the flesh-warm air beside his face.
Perhaps he'd simply shake the man awake
and whisper, *I love you.* He might go further.
He doesn't know. But love is even more dangerous
than lust or force. It can lead you to do
nothing. Lead you to abstinence and silence.
Lead you, Ashpenaz, a man I envy
because I envy the driven. They've ceased
to agonize on what or why — just how.
But passion stops at nothing. There are women
whom I, in awe of waking, have watched sleep
and I have ached to hold my face
down next to theirs, almost touching, and breathe
their breath, which will be sour with sleep,
raw in the heat of dreams. But if I breathed it,
I'd want to kiss their parted, sleeping lips
and if they wakened to the kiss I'd want
to love them as I loved another woman.

Sloping above me like the ceiling of
an attic room, sweat streaming from her face
and onto mine, she laughed, and as she came
she whispered in my ear, *Goddamn you! God-
damn you! Goddamn you!* And though I didn't want
the love to understand, I understood.
We grew so strange in love and understanding
we couldn't risk talk. But Ashpenaz
risks his life to bring Daniel water, bread,
fresh plums, and, once, a spider trapped in amber.
Even these are nothing. Trash. As gifts, he brings
his dreams. And it is terrible to see
the prophet fall on them each day, savage
as a street dog during siege or famine.
And if the frightened eunuch will not talk
Daniel grabs him by the hand and cries,
You dreamed this! This is what you dreamed!
And then he tells the eunuch what it means,
and in detail.

     My love, we were more careful.
Perhaps too careful. I no longer know.
Each night sleep lifted us up off the sheets
where we lay side by fragile, sleeping side
lost separately in the same domain of fierce
outlandish couplings with other people —
mothers, strangers, men. We have a need
to learn, in there, the loves forbidden here.
But what we learn we may not want to know.

Returning home, still dazzled at the crossing,
we now and then forget we've left our dreams
whose outlaw grace allows us anything,
and we are slightly strange to one another,
formal and wary, not sure what we might do.
The eunuch knows what he is doing. After
long hours divulging dreams, he walks alone
into the cool air of the palace hall.
The vessels the slaves fill with water sway
above his head, cooling the rooms. In summer
they lift them down three times a day, then cart
them to the river, a dozen at a time.
Two hundred vessels. Clay. They break at least
one jug a day. They're beaten for their lack
of grace, their clumsiness. And they should be
because we must be careful in a world
that breaks so easily beneath our hands,
even for Ashpenaz — a careful man.
This eunuch from four thousand years ago
who may have never lived, this man I love,
walks home beneath the fragile, hanging jars,
heading toward sleep as some men head to work,
returning to his dreams as if he'd lost
something in there, where each half of the mind
pitches itself against the other half
with so much rage it is both bite and kiss,
devour and complete. Toward dawn they tear
themselves apart — awed, dumb, and unappeased —
and Ashpenaz throws on his robe and runs
to tell it all to Daniel, who already knows.

Consider

You have considered the lilies of the field,
how they do nothing for their splendor
and how they shine like moons upon their stalks,
arrayed in the exacting glory of the sun.
Consider now the mosses of the cypress swamp,
the great droop-headed grasses of the salt marsh,
and how, beneath the shadowed pastels
of the wetland flowers, there lingers a hint of violet
that fades in full light, whitens and dies
like a sin you are especially partial to
because it makes your life more intricate
and somehow better. Consider, too, the various lights
that outlast the last, hard leg of the pilgrimage
through leaf and branch, moss, mist, haze, and gnats,
are rare and changed, softened with impurities,
and should be blessed each with a proper name.
In the sun-bright fields it's just called light
because it's known there only in its scouring brightness.
Consider the dream I dreamt last night of Christ
glowing in holiness, as metal in a forge
will pulsate red, yellow, and finally white
before it starts to lose its this-world shape.
He asked me to bathe his burning face
and soften the radiance that was killing him,
and I led him to the marsh and immersed him,
almost vanishing in the steam that rose around us.
Consider: from the reeds close at hand the marsh hen lunges,
a blast of stubby wings and dangling legs,
so awkward she soon relinquishes the sky,
flashing the patch of white beneath her tail

as she bolts between the tassels of marsh grass.
And down the random corridor of water oaks
beckons the hollow, two-note fluting of an owl.

IV

SAINTS AND
STRANGERS

1. At the Piano

One night two hunters, drunk, came in the tent.
They fired their guns and stood there stupidly
as Daddy left the pulpit, stalked toward them,
and slapped them each across the mouth. He split
one's upper lip.
                        They beat him like a dog.
They propped their guns against the center pole,
rolled up their sleeves as Daddy stood and preached
about the desecration of God's house.
They punched him down, took turns kicking his ribs,
while thirty old women and sixteen men
sat slack-jawed in their folding chairs and watched.
Just twelve, not knowing what to do, I launched
into "Amazing Grace" — the only hymn
I knew by heart — and everybody sang.
We sang until the hunters grew ashamed
— or maybe tired — and left, taking their guns,
their faces red and gleaming from the work.

They got three years suspended sentence each
and Daddy got another tale of how
Christians are saints and strangers in the world.
I guess he knows. He said that I'd done right
to play the song. God's music saved his life.
But I don't know. I couldn't make a guess.
Can you imagine what it means to be
just barely twelve, a Christian and a girl,
and see your father beaten to a pulp?
Neither can I, God knows, and I was there

in the hot tent, beneath the mildewed cloth,
breathing the August, Alabama air,
and I don't know what happened there, to me.
I told this to my second husband, Jim.
We were just dating then. I cried a lot.
He said, *Hush, dear, at least your father got*
a chance to turn all four of his cheeks.
I laughed. I knew, right then, I was in love.
But still I see that image of my father,
his weight humped on his shoulders as he tried
to stand, and I kept plunging through the song
so I could watch my hands and not his face,
which was rouged crimson with red clay and blood.

2. Eve's Sin

Some summer nights when we were on the road
we slept in sleeping bags inside the tent —
money. I'd listen to mosquitoes sing,
how they go oddly silent as they strike.
If I were bored enough I'd let them land
and fill themselves with blood. Then I'd decide
if I would let them go or slap them dead,
knowing I'd wake to find the purple flecks
smudged randomly across my neck and arms.

As I removed my dress to go to sleep,
I saw my underpants were dark with blood.
There wasn't any pain but I was scared.
I called, *Daddy?* He said, *Hush, Marie.*
I said, *I'm bleeding, Daddy.* He was strange,
yet happy too. He held my hands and said,
*This happens to all little girls. I should
have mentioned it. You'll bleed like this each month —
about five days. It's . . .* He paused and thought,
and that long pause scared me so bad I cried
until I vomited. It sounded so
illogical. I was convinced that I
was dying. It took me years to figure out
that he'd almost explained the sin of Eve
which every woman suffers for. But that
was years later. He rocked me like a child.
He whispered, *Hush now, Baby. Hush yourself,*
kissed my drenched cheeks, and zipped me in the bag,
an undershirt clenched hard between my thighs.

3. Where the River Jordan Ends

She put two flowered hair clasps in my hair.
They held. I was amazed. Though Daddy thought
I should be wearing ribbons on my head
he couldn't make them stay. One Christmas Day
he saved the ribbons left from opening gifts
and looped them through my curls. We went to church,
where Aunt Bess snickered, picked them from my hair
and off my neck. She told Daddy, *Jerome,*
she's festooned like a nigger Christmas tree.
But Mrs. Shores knew everything! She smiled
and smoothed my hair around the flowered clasps.
Her husband had invited Daddy down
to preach a week's revival at his church,
and she, since I was almost thirteen, let me
drink coffee when the men were off at work.

Their son took me and Sis into the church.
We ran around the aisles till we got tired,
then shucked our shoes and socks, sat on the rail,
and dangled feet into the River Jordan —
a painting on the wall that seemed to flow
into the baptistery. We splashed around,
got wet, then stripped down to our birthday suits,
and leapt into the font. We went berserk.
We were cannonballing off the rail
when Daddy threw the double doors apart.
We jumped into the font and held our breaths.
When I came up, Daddy was standing there,
waiting. I flinched. Instead he touched my cheek:

Put on your clothes, Elizabeth Marie.
And then I saw the tears. I cried all day.
That night as I sat staring at the wall
behind my father, where the Jordan ends,
I heard God's voice and went to be immersed,
trembling and happy in a paper robe,
and Daddy hugged my body to his chest.
I left a wet, dark shadow on his suit.
I wanted to be saved again. Again.

4. Loose Change

We'd sip our water and wait till supper came,
then he'd return thanks. It was never quick
or done by rote. It was heartfelt — and loud —
while everybody in the truck stop watched.
They tried to do it secretly, the way
you look at cripples, retards, droolers, freaks.
I'd raise my head and watch them watching us,
and once, seeing my head unbowed, he said,
Elizabeth Marie, please close your eyes.
He says that we are strangers here on earth
and it is true I've never felt at home.
In Denver, once, a man asked me the way
to Mile High Stadium, and though I'd been
in town almost two years and had a job
I said, *I'm a stranger here myself,*
amazed at what was coming from my lips.
Are you okay? he asked. How could I say
that I'd been talking bad theology?
But it was worse for Daddy, I suspect.
At least I watched the world and tried to make
accommodation. Since he wouldn't tip
I lifted loose change from the offering plate
to slip onto the table as we left.
Staring right at the waitress, I would think,
Take this, you slut, I've stolen it for you.

5.   The Southern Crescent Was On Time

I played piano while my daddy knelt,
unlaced their shoes, and washed the clean pink feet
they'd washed before they'd come to have them washed.
He never just slopped water on the feet
like some men do. Instead he'd lift each foot,
working the soapy rag between their toes
with such relentless tenderness the boys
would giggle, girls would blush, and women sigh.
And though the feet looked clean to begin with,
when he was done the water was as black
as crankcase oil.
                    And then he'd preach, preach hard.
Black suit, black tie, white shirt gone limp with heat,
he'd slap the pulpit and a spray of sweat
would fly into the air. He'd wipe his brow,
letting the silence work into the crowd,
and then start low, or with — almost — a shout.
I never could guess which. His face would gleam
with sweat. It was as if he were, each night,
baptizing himself from the inside out.

As you drive home tonight, he'd say, *a truck*
a diesel truck,
               might cross into your lane
and you would die apart from God,
                                   unsaved.
One night a pair of twins sat in this tent
and each one heard God speaking to his heart.

One twin came forward to be saved,
                              and one
stayed in his seat,
                resisted God's free grace.
He needed time to think — or so he thought —
but you can't know when God will take you back.
The earth is not our home. We're passing through.
That night
            as they drove to the Dairy Queen
their brand-new car stalled on the railroad track.
That night
            the Southern Crescent was on time.
One went to heaven with his loving God,
and we know where the other went,
                              don't we?
The place where you are bathed in clinging fire
and it will last forever,
                    burning, burning,
and you will beg to die.
                    But you can't die
because, poor fool,
                you are already dead.

He'd wipe his forehead with a handkerchief.

If you should die tonight where will your soul
reside for all eternity?
                    In fire?
Or will you sit, in grace, at God's right hand?

Come up for God's free cleansing love.
                              Come up.
Let Jesus take your sins away.
                         Come up.

They'd come and Daddy would dunk them on the spot
so they could face the family car in peace.
Waiting for them as they lurched down the aisle,
he stood, head bowed, arms raised above his head,
and I would play until his hands came down
and touched his belt. And once I played
twenty-two verses of "Just As I Am"
while Daddy stood there stubbornly, arms raised,
waiting for God to move their hardened hearts.
I prayed that someone would be saved. My sweat
dripped on my hands. My fingers cramped
and skittered on the keys, then I passed out.

                    When I came to,
the crowd was gone and Daddy's coat was tucked
beneath my head. He rubbed my arms, rolling
the limp flesh back and forth between his hands.
His eyes were focused past the empty chairs
and out the door. His lips moved silently
so I could tell he was praying for me.
But what, I didn't ask or want to know.

6.   A Kiss in Church

I had to giggle at the way he sang
"Amazing Grace" like Donald Duck. And once,
while everybody's head was bowed, he kissed
me on the mouth. But Daddy saw the kiss
and later, after church, he yelled at me.
I was too big — too old — for him to slap.
He wouldn't stop yelling. I wouldn't cry
or say that I'd done wrong. Next thing I knew
I was married. Though Daddy says I was,
I don't remember being asked. Bud was
a handsome boy. So Daddy could be right.
But for the longest time after I left
I kept this scene to jab into my heart:
Bud sitting, dirty, at the kitchen table,
his flannel sleeves rolled past his elbows.
He's giving me that hangdog look of his
as I stand in the doorway, adamant,
my second baby straddling my hip.
How can he be so meaningless, who once
was everything. And what am I to him?
Nothing. I hope nothing. Nothing at all.

7. *Glossolalia*

There was one sagging bed, all his. We slept
on quilts — a pallet in the living room —
and listened to his shallow, rasping breaths
assert themselves against the growl and suck
of diesels on the interstate. They made
the whole house shake. While Sis was off at work
I wiped dried Maalox from his lips, fed him,
and prayed as best I could. And I'd call home
and talk for hours to the girls and Jim
until I couldn't tell the phone calls from
the prayers. Daddy's speech returned to English
and we could understand, at last, the words,
which up till then had been a random, wild
intensity of esses. It sounded like
the tongues of fire, the glossolalia
that slithers off the otherworldly tongues
of people baptized in the Holy Ghost.
His demons suddenly were visible
and he'd been talking to them in a tongue
we couldn't understand. It frightened us.
It was like we were children once again
and there was Daddy once again endowed
with knowledge of a world we couldn't see.

When he walked off, the sheriff brought him back
and helped me tuck him in. Over iced tea,
he said that Daddy'd run through Kroger's, shouting,
and pointing out the demons. One lady screamed
when Daddy shouted in her face, *My God!*

One's chewing on your ear! The sheriff thought
that was a hoot. He laughed and slapped his thigh.
At supper Sis got mad and screamed at me
for letting him stray off. I let it slide
and passed the meat. That night, rising to pee,
I found her curled up on Daddy's bed.
He was asleep and she was sleeping too,
her face unaging as she shed the world,
and she was shining: light trickled down her face,
her cheeks. It shone like streams of molten solder.
Silver would sound more beautiful and it
was beautiful. It took my breath away.
But I have never seen molten silver.
Or molten glass.

              I made my mind up then
she didn't have the strength to care for Daddy.
It was my turn. Before I left, we sold
the loaded truck, the folding chairs, the tent.
Almost nine hundred bucks. The root of evil.
Enough for her to let her sainthood go.
And if I wouldn't change a thing — not this,
not anything — is that a lack of faith?
Too much imagination? Not enough?

8. Saints and Strangers

You teach a Baptist etiquette, she turns
Episcopalian. I did. It's calm.
And Daddy, who shudders when I take the host,
stays home and worships with the TV set.
He's scared to leave the house. Incontinence.
When he's wet himself, he lets us know
by standing grimly at our bedroom door
and reading from his Bible. We think about
a nursing home. If I put on Ray Charles
he huffs around the house and says, *Marie,*
that nigger jungle-thumping hurts my head.
But these are little things. In many ways
the stroke has helped. He's gentle with the girls.
For hours he'll ride them horsy on his knees.
Still, there are those damn demons. Mine are blue,
Jim's red. He whispers demons to the girls
and gets them so they don't know what to think
of us. Beth's asthma starts. I tell the girls,
You play pretend, don't you? Well, you can stop.
But Paw-paw can't. He always plays pretend.
They seem to understand. In some ways, though,
I think he's even purer now — a saint
of all his biases, almost beyond
the brute correction of our daily lives.
Strangeness is part of it. And rage and will.
There's something noble in that suffering
and something stupid too. I'm not a saint,
of course, but as a child I had a rage
I've lost to age, to sex, to understanding,

which takes the edge off everything. Perhaps
it's my metabolism cooling down.
Who knows? One glory of a family is
you'd never choose your kin and can't unchoose
· your daddy's hazel eyes — no more than you
could unchoose your hand. You get to be,
in turn, someone you'd never choose to be.
When feeling strong, I'll ask him to give thanks.
If he goes on too long, I say amen
and pass whatever bowl is near at hand.
Jim carves the meat, the girls reach for their tea,
and Daddy takes the bowl and helps his plate.